THE BUSIN

Biz of Time Publishing bizoftime.com

ISBN: 978-1-7352375-0-3

Discounts are available for books ordered in bulk.

Inquire at bizoftime.com

Biz of Time Publishing
130 W. Main Street Suite 144 #408, Collegeville, PA 19426

TABLE OF CONTENTS

This book is dedicated to my daughter. I love you so much and I am so proud of you.

For anyone who reads this book: You can, and you should, enjoy your life.

Never let anyone tell you otherwise.

What is "The Business of Time"?

The Business of Time has three main principles.

1. The first principle is to maximize your earnings by increasing your personal value. By doing so, you can potentially minimize your working hours. This applies whether you work for yourself or work for others. Maximizing your earnings is the first step towards giving yourself the ability to choose to work as much or as little as you *choose* to, provided your personal expenses are not excessive.
2. The second principle is to have alternative options for earning income, where you do not have to physically work to still earn for yourself. Creating passive and/or residual income, and controlling/managing your retirement income, can substantially reduce the amount of years you need to spend physically working. This allows you to spend your time enjoying life, instead of having to physically work more hours/years.
3. The third principle is to understand how valuable your time is. Every individual has the same twenty-four hours in a day. What you do in those hours has a direct effect on your mental health and overall well-being. If you believe that your time is valuable, you may change your outlook about the things you do in your personal/professional time.

Time is the most undervalued asset that we all possess. We cannot physically “buy time”, nor can time be recreated. The ability to choose what we want to do with our time, as opposed to spending years of our lives working out of necessity, is a choice that many people would appreciate. Unfortunately, many people currently believe that they do not have that choice. This book was written to help you understand your options, so that you can eventually *choose* how *you* wish to spend your time.

One of the purposes of this book is to offer perspective about how valuable your time is. If you believe your time is valuable, your attitude regarding the amount of time you spend doing certain activities may change. Additionally, this book is to enlighten you about your ability to *choose* how you wish to spend your time. Many people spend most of their lives working out of necessity, and spend their time doing things they are not passionate about, because they are unaware of their earning options. Once you investigate the avenues available for you to earn income, your perspective about how you are currently earning your income may change as well.

If you have ever heard the phrase “time is money”, but you did not understand the meaning of the phrase, that was also my experience with the phrase for many years. I thought “time is money” only applied to the wealthy, because I had typically only heard wealthy people mention the phrase repeatedly. As I grew older though, the definition of the phrase came into focus. What I began to realize is that from the moment you are old enough to work, the concept of “time is money” applies to all of us.

Everyone is in The Business of Time, regardless of what your title or profession is. If you are a working-class individual, every minute of your day is monetized whether you realize it or not. Every working-class person around the world has a different value for their working time, and they may all value their own personal time in different ways as well. If you ask someone how much they'd like to work vs. how much they'd like to earn, a frequent answer might be that they'd like to earn as much as possible while working as little as possible. If this is your goal as well, this book can help you achieve your goal.

I wrote this book because I spent 20 years working out of necessity before I made a choice to take control of my life. During a ten-year period of those 20 years I had earned over one million dollars (gross earnings), yet I was not close to retirement nor did I feel comfortable financially. That may sound odd to some people, but this book will explain how and why that is a reality for more people than you may realize.

The main reason why I felt financially uncomfortable was because I did not educate myself about money until later in life. Some of the uncomfortable feelings were self-inflicted, due to living beyond my means. Had I known some of the principles taught in this book earlier in life though, I may not have been living beyond my means at all. I did not realize how important managing my retirement earnings, separately from the money I utilized for everyday expenditures, was until much later in life. By doing so, I gained a clearer perspective about how to retire comfortably while working at my own pace on a day-to-day basis.

I believe if most people were given the choice of whether they would like to spend their time working, or just simply enjoying life, that the majority of people would choose to do things that they enjoy with their time. That is why retirement is discussed at length in this book. You can retire when you no longer need to work to afford your lifestyle. Also, you do not have to retire to live life how you see fit. If you enjoy working, and you see no need to retire, then you can continue to work for as long as you would like. It would be your *choice* though, not something you do out of necessity.

Unfortunately, many people's reality is that money does have a role in their overall happiness. Money alone cannot buy happiness in many situations. Money can help lead to more freedom though, and freedom can assist with the feeling of happiness. If you understand this, you can begin to understand the concept of The Business of Time.

This book is not going to discuss how to manage your expenses. You can find many helpful articles about managing your expenses on the internet, which can be useful in conjunction with the content you will learn here. Keep this in mind though: you can only save as much as you earn, and that is why we are going to focus on maximizing your earnings and controlling the money you earn. It is not a bad idea to minimize your expenses, but you are free to live your lifestyle how you see fit. Although this book frequently talks about the US dollar (because that is my country of origin), the principles in this book apply globally.

There are three lessons I would like for you to learn from this book. The first lesson is to maximize your earnings, you must increase your personal value.

Maximizing your earnings can minimize the amount of time you need to spend working, so we will discuss how you can increase your personal value at length in this book.

The second lesson is that if you focus on finding ways to earn money, without having to physically work to earn it, you can alleviate some stress from your life. The ability to support yourself and your family financially, without having to physically work, can make life easier for you. The reason is because you will have more time to live your life as you see fit.

The third, and most important, lesson I would like for you to take from this book is that your time is valuable. If you wish to achieve certain goals in life, you will most likely require *time* to achieve your goals. Perhaps you are less focused on earning money and more focused on spending time with your family. The amount of time you work has a direct impact on the amount of time you can spend with your family, because we all have the same twenty-four hours available to us each day. If you consider your time valuable, and maximize your earnings during your working hours, you can spend more time with your family and less time working.

We have all made the mistake of taking time for granted. My hope is that you can begin to manage your time efficiently after reading this book, if you are not doing so already. Whether you enjoy working and want to work all the time, or you enjoy spending your time doing anything *but* work, let it be your choice to make. Thank you for investing your time to read this book, and I hope you enjoy.

I. The Road to Retirement

"Before you can arrive, you must first know where you are going"

Having only one source of income can make for a long and hard road to retirement. This is especially true if you do not save for retirement, separate from your standard savings. If you carefully invest and manage your retirement earnings, that can become another source of income for you. That will be discussed later in this book; however, many people spend their entire lives working only one job at a time and *hope* that they can retire at a decent age. In this chapter, we will discuss how difficult it can be to retire with just one (or even two) incomes in a household with children. Even if you earn what many people believe to be a healthy amount of money, you can end up working well into your senior years if you are not focusing on retirement.

If you plan on only having one source of income for your entire life, $100,000 dollars per year may not be a lot of money. To the average working American, $100,000 dollars per year might seem like a lot of money. When you compare your net income to your actual cost of living though, regardless of your living situation, you will find that $100,000 per year may just barely cover your expenses. Below you will find an example of the cost of living in America with one child and multiple children. We will then compare what happens to your income after your monthly expenses are tallied up over a 30-year period, starting at age 30.

<u>Annual income = $100,000 dollars</u>
$100,000 gross annual pay * 34% average total payroll deductions = $34,000 annual deductions
$100,000 gross annual pay - $34,000 annual deductions = $66,000 annual net (take-home) income
$66,000 annual net income / 12 months = *$5,500 monthly net income*

Expenses
Average shelter expense = *$1,300* monthly. This assumes either a $1,300 rent with utilities included for a two-bedroom apartment or a $1,000 mortgage payment including taxes on a single family home with $300 per month in utilities.
Average transportation expense (car payment, insurance, gas) = *$500* monthly.
Average mobile phone expense = *$100* monthly.
Average cable/TV/internet expense = *$100* monthly.
Average food expense = *$1,000* monthly.
Average entertainment expense (movies, date night, night life etc.) = *$500* monthly.
Average child care expense (daycare, school activities, college fund, etc.) *$1,000* monthly.

Total average expenses in a one child household = ***$4,500*** *average monthly expense*

In the following expense vs. income example, we will compare the $100,000 income to the expenses in a one, two, and three child household. We will increase the overall household expense by $500 per child for example purposes only. If we compare the income to the expenses over a 30-year period, starting at age 30, this is what the calculations would be:

One child household
$5,500 monthly net income - $4,500 average monthly expense = *$1,000* possible monthly savings
$1,000 possible monthly savings * 12 months in a year = $12,000 annual possible savings
$12,000 * 30 years = ***$360,000*** actual savings by age 60

Two child household
$5,500 monthly net income - $5,000 average monthly expense = *$500* possible monthly savings
$500 possible monthly savings * 12 months in a year = $6,000 annual possible savings
$6,000 * 30 years = ***$180,000*** actual savings by age 60

Three child household
$5,500 monthly net income - $5,500 average monthly expense = *$0* monthly savings
$0 possible monthly savings * 12 months in a year = $0 annual savings
$0 * 30 years = ***$0*** savings by age 60

You can see how quickly savings can decrease for each child you add into the equation. In each of these examples, you would be 60 years old and hopefully you would be getting ready to retire. Multiple sources say that the average amount required to retire in America today is around, or above, one million dollars. In this example, you can see that even in a one child household you would be well below the million-dollar mark by the time you are 60 years old.

A few more factors to consider: The original expenses in the equation did not take into consideration the cost of your shelter expense potentially increasing to add bedrooms for each child. Other expenses that were not discussed were out-of-pocket healthcare costs and emergency expenses, which could include things like home repairs, car repairs, family emergencies, etc. If we assume out-of-pocket healthcare costs were only $250 per month and emergency expenses were also only $250 per month (these figures may be low, especially for homeowners or families with multiple children, compared to today's cost of living), that would be an additional $500 monthly expense to consider. If we added a $500 monthly expense to each of the above examples you would have less to retire with in a one child household, you would have no savings in a two child household and you would be heavily in debt in a three child household by the time you're 60 years old.

You may be asking yourself by now "What if I make $100,000 per year and my spouse works as well?" That is a great question, we will examine that as well. We can assume your spouse also adds $50,000 into the equation, so you have a combined household income of $150,000 annually (or you each make $75,000 annually). This is far more than the average American household earns, but we will examine this scenario for example purposes. This example will include the additional $500 in expenses for emergency expenses and/or out of pocket medical expenses.

Annual income = $150,000
$150,000 gross annual pay * 34% average total payroll deductions = $51,000 annual deductions
$150,000 gross annual pay - $51,000 annual deductions = $99,000 annual net (take-home) income
$99,000 annual net income / 12 months = *$8,250 monthly net income*

Expenses

One child household

$4,500 monthly expenses + $500 monthly for out-of-pocket healthcare/emergencies = *$5,000* monthly

Two child household

$5,000 monthly expenses + $500 monthly for out-of-pocket healthcare/emergencies = *$5,500* monthly

Three child household

$5,500 monthly expenses + $500 monthly for out-of-pocket healthcare/emergencies = *$6,000* monthly

One child household – income vs. expenses

$8,250 monthly net income - $5,000 average monthly expense = *$3,250* possible monthly savings
$3,250 possible monthly savings * 12 months in a year = $39,000 annual possible savings
$39,000 * 30 years = ***$1,170,000*** actual savings

Two child household – income vs. expenses

$8,250 monthly net income - $5,500 average monthly expense = *$2,750* possible monthly savings
$2,750 possible monthly savings * 12 months in a year = $33,000 annual possible savings
$33,000 * 30 years = ***$990,000*** actual savings

Three child household – income vs. expenses

$8,250 monthly net income - $6,000 average monthly expense = *$2,250* possible monthly savings
$2,250 possible monthly savings * 12 months in a year = $27,000 annual possible savings
$27,000 * 30 years = ***$810,000*** actual savings

Based on this example, you may have found your answer to retirement. You might be thinking, "If my spouse and I just make $150,000 consistently for the next 30 years, we'll have solid savings and the next

5 years or so to save and retire at 65". Possibly. We can expand on this thought and examine this from a slightly more realistic perspective, to see how that would look as well.

There are a lot of factors that are not being considered in the original expense estimates. The first missing factor is that the average American car payment on a used car is around $390 per month. If you multiply that times two (two drivers in the household), plus insurance and gas on both cars, your average transportation expense is closer to or over $1,000 per month. Next is out-of-pocket healthcare costs and emergency expenses. The more children you have, the more these expenses increase, and the original estimates may have been low already. Also, other factors that are not being taken into consideration include the cost of a potential household expense increase to accommodate for a second or third child, increased taxes on your home, and general inflation. These estimates also assume that you and your spouse will make $150,000 *consistently* for 30 years with absolutely no loss in job, wages, or either party wanting to retire early. That may be a bit unrealistic. For argument's sake, we can assume that you can make $150,000 consistently over that period, but we will also take the other factors into consideration.

In this example we are going to slightly increase the housing expense to $1,500 in each scenario, assuming you planned for more than one child. We are going to increase the transportation expense to $800 per month for two cars, and we are going to factor more realistic out-of-pocket healthcare and emergency costs of $1,000 per month across the board. This equals a $1,500 increase from the original estimates and is a bit closer to an actual representation of your possible expenses. In many states, especially some of the more metropolitan areas, these costs may still be low compared to the actual cost of living. Below is an example of what the calculations are with the updated expenses:

<u>One child household</u>
$8,250 monthly net income - $6,000 average monthly expense = *$2,250* possible monthly savings
$2,250 possible monthly savings * 12 months in a year = $27,000 annual possible savings
$27,000 * 30 years = ***$810,000*** actual savings

<u>Two child household</u>
$8,250 monthly net income - $6,500 average monthly expense = *$1,750* possible monthly savings
$1,750 possible monthly savings * 12 months in a year = $21,000 annual possible savings
$21,000 * 30 years = ***$630,000*** actual savings

<u>Three child household</u>
$8,250 monthly net income - $7,000 average monthly expense = *$1,250* possible monthly savings
$1,250 possible monthly savings * 12 months in a year = $15,000 annual possible savings
$15,000 * 30 years = ***$450,000*** actual savings

As you can see, even if you and your spouse were to make $150,000 consistently for 30 years with just two children, you would still be below the minimum of one million dollars to retire with by the time you're age 60. $810,000 is a good retirement fund at 60 years old if you only had one child, but this is also assuming your home payment or mortgage payment is not higher than estimated. Or that your mobile phone expense or food expense is not higher than estimated. Or that you will not suffer a loss in wages at any point over 30 years. Not to mention that $150,000 annually is substantially higher than the average American household income. This also does not take into consideration the fact that none of these figures accounted for incidentals like haircuts, clothing, etc.

Nothing that was said in this chapter is meant to scare you or make you feel hopeless about your future. Later in this book, we will discuss alternate ways to earn income and the impact that has on your road to retirement. Also, your expenses may be lower depending on where you live, and you are able to save more than the estimates seen in this chapter. If you do not currently have children, that will substantially reduce your expenses as well (I am not advocating for you to avoid having children, just stating a fact). Your job may also offer a 401K match or a pension, which can help towards the amount of money you have available when you are ready to retire.

All of this is to say that your financial future is not bleak. It can be difficult to retire though, and live comfortably, if you plan on only relying on one source of income during your entire career.

The purpose of what was said in this chapter is to enlighten you about how difficult it can be to retire in America (or worldwide). A large percentage of people are unaware of how difficult it is to comfortably retire in America or anywhere in the world. Regardless of when you read this and what your current career level is, this book will hopefully offer some perspective that you may not have thought about previously.

By now, you might be asking “what does any of this have to do with The Business of Time?” Good question. Before we examine the value of your time, we must first have a realistic understanding of how much money is required to live comfortably and hopefully one day retire at a reasonable age. Throughout the course of this book your income/wages are going to be compared to the amount of time you will spend working. Your work/home life balance will also be discussed because this is a key component of your quality of life.

One of the main purposes of this book is for you to understand how valuable your time is, so you can appropriately assess where you want to spend your time. Once you assess where you want to spend your time, you can then ultimately manage your time and your own personal mental health. Money is not everything, however it can contribute to your health, quality of life and overall happiness. Therefore, it is important to consider the impact money can have when evaluating the value of your time. Once you understand the role money plays in your overall personal happiness, you can then begin to determine what your time is worth. Once you are maximizing the earnings you make during your working hours, you can then begin to manage your time in a way that you find suitable for your lifestyle.

II. The Time Value of Money

In the previous chapter we discussed the road to retirement. In the introduction, we discussed why everyone is in The Business of Time. In this chapter, we are going to tie the two concepts together and begin to explain how valuable your time is.

Regardless of how you earn your income, there is a time value to the wages you earn. Whether you are paid hourly, salary, commissions, by contract, or any combination of those methods, the time you spend working has a direct correlation on what your time is worth. Here are a few examples:

*Hourly employee makes $15 per hour and works 40 hours per week. That is $600 per week and $31,200 annually (52 weeks each year * $600). This employee works 2080 hours in a year (52 weeks * 40 hours) so if you divide their annual pay by the number of hours they work, it is still $15 per hour.*

*Salary employee makes $31,200 per year (annually) but works 50 hours per week. This is still $600 per week, but this employee works 2600 hours (52 weeks * 50 hours) in a year. If you divide their annual pay by the number of hours they work, they actually earn $12 per hour.*

Salary employee makes $104,000 annually and works 40 hours per week. That is $2000 per week and they work 2080 hours in a year. If you divide their annual pay by the number of hours in the year, they make $50 per hour.

Commissioned employee makes $104,000 annually and works 50 hours per week. That is still $2000 per week but they work 2600 hours in a year. If you divide their annual pay by the number of hours they work, it equates to $40 per hour.

You can examine your own personal wages from this viewpoint and make your own determination of what you actually earn per hour. In each of these examples, every employee worked a minimum of 40 hours per week and they all had a different monetary value for their time. Regardless of the number of hours worked, when you compare the earnings of both employees in the $31,200 example and both employees in the $104,000 example, their earnings are the same. However, in both examples the employees who worked 50 hours per week ended up working 520 more hours per year. If you divide the 520 hours per year by 24 hours in a day, the people working the extra 520 hours end up working a full 21 days more for the same money. That is three more full weeks of work each year. Considering there are only 52 weeks in a year, that is a substantial amount of time.

Why is this important? Simply put, the more hours you spend working, the less time you have available to do things that you enjoy. This might not be a problem if you enjoy your work, but it could be problematic for your mental health if you dislike your job/career.

Even though you may be making $104,000 annually, you may feel as though you don't have enough time to spend with your spouse and children, or enough time to go to the gym, or just have any type of social life. This is where money plays an important role in your overall mental health.

Depending on how much time you spend working to make a living, and how much money you earn annually (per year), you may have an unbalanced lifestyle and be generally unhappy. While you may be doing so to support your family, this could be toxic for you and the people around you. The Business of Time was written to offer perspective about your options. Typically, if people are feeling "stuck" in a situation, it is because they are unaware of the options available to them to earn money outside of physically working. We will discuss this subject in future chapters, in addition to how to maximize your earnings so you do not have to work the additional 520 hours per year (as discussed in the previous examples).

In the next chapter, we will discuss the value of your personal time. There is no right or wrong answer regarding how you spend your personal time if you are comfortable with the results. If you are feeling unhappy or uncomfortable though, you may want to examine your situation and determine why you are feeling this way. If the reason is work-related, you may be working too much or do not like your job/career for one reason or another. In future chapters we will discuss alternate ways for you to earn money. If you can earn passive/residual income, you may not feel bound to a job or a career that you dislike.

III. The Value of Personal Time

If you pay attention to the internet, there are many posts and articles about what you "should" be doing in your personal time. Many of these articles are irrelevant because they do not apply to your personal lifestyle. The reason these articles are irrelevant is because happiness, and/or productivity, are matters of perspective. In this chapter, we will discuss an example of how two people choose to spend their personal time. The example is meant to illustrate how two people with the same job can spend their personal time very differently. We will then discuss the affect your lifestyle has on your overall happiness.

Example
Salesperson A works 40 hours per week. In their personal time they enjoy working out, playing sports and spending quality time with their family. Salesperson A sells 10 items per month and earns an average of $4,000 per month.

Salesperson B works 40 hours per week. In their personal time they enjoy working out and spending quality time with their family, but Salesperson B also spends a few hours each week promoting themselves on social media. Salesperson B sells 18 items per month and earns an average of $7,800 per month.

Which person would you rather be? If you are looking at this solely from a monetary perspective, you may say you would want to be Salesperson B.

Both salespeople lead similar lifestyles, but Salesperson B earns almost double what Salesperson A earns per month. This is where personal time can become a complicated matter. Salesperson A could be semi-retired; or perhaps they are a young person who has no bills and $4,000 per month is plenty for them to get by. Salesperson B may have an expensive car and/or house and needs to make $7,800 per month just to survive. Or it is possible that Salesperson B has no debt and just enjoys their job as a salesperson.

The value of your personal time depends on your lifestyle. There is no right or wrong answer to how you spend your personal time if you are satisfied with your life. There are some people who have no problem working during their free time and are satisfied (or happy) with their lives. There are some people who have plenty of free time but are very unhappy with their lives. There are also some people who are earning average incomes and are completely happy with their lives as well.

Being honest with yourself is a great starting point toward achieving happiness. It is important to understand who you are as a person, and what you are comfortable with, when examining your lifestyle. If you are happy to work extra and providing for your family makes you feel good, there is nothing wrong with that. There is also nothing wrong with doing things that you enjoy in your life, provided you are not feeling as though there are other areas of your life that are suffering and/or causing you stress.

If you believe money is the reason why you feel unhappy or unsettled in life, the Business of Time was written to help you. In future chapters we will discuss how to maximize your earnings during your working hours. By doing so, you can give yourself the ability to choose how you wish to spend your personal time. We will also discuss ways to earn money without having to physically work, which can also provide additional income or allow you to spend more time doing things that you enjoy.

What you do with your personal time is entirely up to you. There are a lot of activities that you can do during your personal time that will not increase your value or that can make you feel invaluable. Something to keep in mind though, is that we all have the same number of hours in a day and a limited amount of time on this earth. When you start to realize that the things you do (or the people around you) are unproductive for you and your mental health, you may start to value your time differently. When you value your time differently, you may choose to spend your time doing things that are more beneficial to you in the time that you have available. That is why being honest with yourself is so important when assessing how to spend your personal time.

In the next chapter, we are going to discuss some skills you can acquire and some activities that you can do to help you build your personal value. Once you have built your personal value, you can then begin to maximize your earnings while you are physically working. When you maximize your earnings, you may not need to work overtime or a second job because you are able to afford your lifestyle. This leads to more time, and you can then choose how you wish to spend that time. Regardless of how you choose to spend your time, the end goal is for you to be able to enjoy life.

Chapter Checklist

In this chapter we discussed how people value their personal time. Are you feeling happy and/or satisfied with your life currently?

- Yes?
- No?

If the answer is no, ask yourself the following:

- What is making you feel unhappy or unsettled?
- Are the reasons money-related? If so, what are you willing to do to change your situation?
- Do you feel as though you are working too much? Or perhaps not enough?
- Have you examined your earnings options yet? (We will discuss this in future chapters)
- Are the activities you do in your personal time affecting your mental health positively or negatively? Are you willing to make changes to improve your situation?
- What are your short-term and long-term goals in life? Would achieving your goals help you feel accomplished and satisfied?
- What would make you happy?

IV. Building Value in Yourself

"Whether you think you can, or you think you can't... You're right" - Henry Ford

In the introduction, we discussed earning as much as possible while working as little as possible. It may sound like a foreign concept to some people and it may sound like a pipe dream to others, but this is many people's reality. The way to make this your reality is by building value in yourself, and this chapter is dedicated to helping you improve your overall value. When you are more valuable, you can choose between working as much or as little as you choose to and earning as much as you need to feel satisfied.

We will start with the basics. To build value in yourself, you must first believe in yourself enough to realize that you can do whatever it is that *you choose.* That is not to say that you should have an unrelenting will to achieve your goal and have tunnel vision about whatever your aspirations are. If you are steadfast (or stubborn) about attempting to achieve something that is not working, there is a very real possibility that you may fail. Failure can be a learning experience. If you fail at something, you will have other opportunities to try again. There are countless examples of successful entrepreneurs who attempted a business and failed, then got it right the second or third time they tried.

Also, you do not have to be an entrepreneur to apply this concept. Perhaps you are in the right industry but in the wrong position/role/employer.

When you find the right fit though, your career can blossom. It can be hard for your career to blossom however, if you do not believe you are able to do so. If you do not believe in yourself yet, you may want to consider contacting a mentor or coach who can help you build self-confidence. Regardless, building value in yourself starts with believing in yourself.

The next step towards building value in yourself is to acquire skills during your lifetime that can help increase your personal value. Sometimes a best practice can be to acquire as many skills as you possibly can. Also, you might only acquire a few skills and master them, but you then become valuable based on your expert knowledge in a particular subject/field. Certain professions require a varied skillset, while others require you to be an expert at only one task. A best practice before deciding which skills you would like to work on would be to research what is required to excel in the industry, or position, you would like to be in. Once you have planned for what is required, you can then begin to learn the necessary skills to be successful. This can be done at any point in life, even if you have already started a career in a different industry.

Another trait that allows you to build value in yourself is the ability to be open-minded (flexible). Throughout the course of your lifetime you will have the opportunity to learn something new almost daily. When life lessons occur, what you do with the information that is presented to you will shape your personality, your personal interactions, and often your ability to earn money. Ask yourself, "Do I have 10 years of experience in my field? Or do I have 1 year of experience 10 times over?" There are many people who learn how to do a task, feel as though they know how to do the task, then stop trying to learn. Unless you are in a field in which you are required to be an expert at only one task, typically the people who choose not to consistently learn and adapt are the people who will not advance. If you are unable to advance in life, you could be forfeiting the option to choose how to spend your time as you see fit.

In the beginning of this chapter we discussed having the ability to choose what you want to do in life. If you choose to be closed-minded, you can take away your ability to choose your path if you would like to further your career within your field. Or if you choose to open your own company, by being closed-minded you could potentially stand in the way of your own success. As a business owner, you can be the roadblock preventing your company from succeeding, regardless of how many talented people you hire.

A strong work ethic can also be helpful towards building value in yourself, however a strong work ethic only goes so far. If you are working hard but not working on skills and tasks that make you more valuable, you may end up working harder but remaining in the same place. Also, there are plenty of people who are successful that other people may deem "lazy". That does not make the person lazy just because it is someone's opinion. The person who is being considered lazy may have found a way to utilize their talents, to maximize their earnings while working as little as possible. Keep this in mind before you pass judgement on others. Sometimes looking at things from a different perspective can help open your eyes to ways to improve yourself, as opposed to simply passing judgement on someone else.

Thus far, everything that has been said in this chapter speaks to a mindset that allows for personal growth. Having a positive mindset that allows for personal growth can be instrumental towards building your personal value. In the next section of this chapter, we will discuss some skills and activities that you can acquire/accomplish over the course of your lifetime that will also help you build your personal value.

Skills and activities to help you build personal value

Throughout your life there will be many opportunities for you to establish yourself. One of the definitions of the word establish is to "achieve permanent acceptance or recognition for". The end of the definition is left open-ended because you can achieve acceptance or recognition for many things. This applies to both working for other people or becoming self-employed. You can establish yourself as an expert in your field of employment and achieve the ability to find employment, at higher wages than your peers. Or you could establish yourself as a thought leader; an individual who people would be willing to pay just to hear your opinions and advice. Regardless of your choice of employment, the skills and activities you will read about in this chapter will help you establish yourself. Once you are established, you will have increased your personal value, and you can then begin maximizing your earnings.

Set goals for yourself

You can start setting goals for yourself at any age and at any point in your life. Some people do not believe in goals, and that is their choice. However, setting goals can help you become motivated if you find yourself lacking motivation. Companies that you work for will often set a goal for you that you may not believe in. If you do not believe in the goal, it can be difficult to find the motivation to achieve that goal. If you are the one setting the goal though, and it is a goal that you believe in, it could help push you to greater heights.

Effective communication

There is a vast difference between talking to someone (or a crowd) and effectively communicating with them. Effective communication means that the people you are speaking to can understand your message. You do not need to be in a leadership position for this to be a crucial element in building your personal value. Effective communication can help you win a job, earn a promotion, recruit others to help you accomplish a task, or just help you to communicate with your family better. If you feel people are not buying into the things that you are saying, ask yourself "am I communicating effectively?" A best practice when it comes to effective communication is to check in with the person or people you are speaking to. Asking a question such as "did that make sense to you?", is an example of a check-in question that can help you determine if you are communicating effectively. Checking in is one method of effective communication. There is also more about this topic on my YouTube channel (Timothy DeJesus).

Build a strong resume

This concept does not just apply to people who are employed by others, and it is not just about what you type on a word processor to describe yourself. Building a strong resume can be essential to your success if you choose to be self-employed as well. This does not mean that if you are self-employed, you are going to create a resume and carry it wherever you go. Building a strong resume, whether you are employed by others or self-employed, means that you are acknowledged/recognized by others for the great service that you provide. For anyone, self-employed or otherwise, building a strong resume is about the skills you acquire throughout your lifetime and what you accomplish by utilizing those skills. Earning accolades speaks directly to the accomplishments you will achieve throughout your career. The accolades you earn can benefit you, because you can then share your accomplishments with employers, etc.

Earn accolades

You can earn people's attention and respect by earning accolades. This can be overlooked in the business world by both employees and employers but is key to building value. Regardless of what field you are in, earning accolades can make you stand out from your peers and competitors. If you enter a job interview as someone who is highly ranked in your industry, you could sway an employer to choose you over another candidate. Or if you are self-employed and you are selling a product or service that is in heavy demand vs. an unknown product or service, you could earn a customer's business instead of your competitor. Some of the most successful people in the world possess a trait called "achievement motivation". That means that money is not the driving factor in their motivation, but rather the accomplishment is the motivation. The accomplishments they achieve, and the recognition they earn, are accolades that can translate into money for them in the future.

Planning

Planning is an essential skill in many facets of life, and a lot can go wrong if you do not have a plan. This goes for general life activities in addition to the workplace. A few examples of how planning can negatively impact you include: entering a job interview unprepared, not preparing for tests, or holding a meeting without an agenda. If you would like to become self-employed someday and need to raise capital for your business, an example of planning would be to prepare a business plan and a presentation prior to meeting with potential investors. If you do not have a business plan, it is almost certain that you will leave an investor's meeting without the capital investment you were hoping for, if any investment at all. You risk wasting time if you fail to plan. You may then spend substantial periods of your life wasting time instead of earning money.

Collaborate with other people

The definition of collaboration is to "work jointly on an activity, especially to produce or create something". Many people think that if they are great at something, they are going to get recognition and achieve great things by default. That works for some people, but generally if you collaborate with others it is easier for you to earn recognition. This happens especially when two or more people, who already have recognition, work together on a project. When two or more people work together on something, they can offer different perspectives. By doing so, they can make the project better by building off each other's ideas and critiquing each other, constructively. They may also enhance each other's brand (corporate or personal) by speaking to each other's audience and gaining notoriety. If you are collaborating, this could lead to new consumers for you and potentially a greater following for your brand.

Build a strong network through your personal brand

Even if you choose not to collaborate with others, you can still build a strong network for yourself. If people recognize who you are, what product or service you are offering, and/or your brand/company, it will be easier for them to buy into you as a person. In today's world, with social media being so prevalent, you can build a strong network quickly through your personal brand. The strength in your relationships, especially on a personal level, can motivate others to help push your brand (personal or otherwise). Being genuinely kind to others and caring about their success can help you achieve great things, instead of only caring about your own personal goals and victories. A best practice to help you network is to learn about any/all social media platforms available to you, and which platforms fit your personal brand best. It can take some time to gain notoriety on social media, so you may want to start sooner than later if you have not started already.

Take care of yourself

Taking care of yourself is not just about eating healthy and exercising. Being active can help you feel better, but you also need to do what is best for your mental health. For some people, diet and exercise may lead to more stress if they are setting their personal goals too high. Taking care of yourself means to set aside time to do the things that you enjoy as a person. That could mean anything, including dedicating more time to spend with your family, planning vacations, or perhaps just setting aside some time for yourself to rest and refocus. Whether you are into video games or yoga, it is important to make sure you are at peace with your own personal schedule. When you do things to reduce the stress factors in your life, that typically leads to a clearer thought process and better decision making.

Learn to effectively negotiate

Some people do not like to negotiate, which is understandable as negotiations can be difficult to navigate at times. Negotiation, however, is an essential skill that is used in almost every facet of our lives. This is not just about the salary at your job. You will find yourself negotiating, on both a personal and professional level, throughout the course of your day without even realizing it. You may negotiate with your children about what they will eat before they earn a snack. You may negotiate with your significant other about who will do certain responsibilities in the household. Or you may need to negotiate your starting salary or a raise with your employer. Regardless, the key to effective negotiation is for both parties to feel satisfied with the result. This especially applies to your earnings and the amount of time you spend working to earn a living. If you feel the money you earn is unequal to the amount of effort required to complete a job, that can leave you feeling dissatisfied. That dissatisfied feeling can affect your well-being and mental health. At the same time, if your employer feels you are overcompensated, they may choose to move on from you in favor of another candidate for less money. Negotiation is a two-way street, but when you learn to negotiate effectively the long-term results can be favorable.

Take ownership (accountability)

You do not need to own a business to take ownership

and/or be accountable. Taking ownership means that you take responsibility for whatever it is you are doing and treat it as though it is your own. This is a crucial element to building your value on many levels. When you take ownership, generally people notice. They see a difference in the quality of your work, and you will feel a difference in your own quality of work. It is also easier to think about possibly becoming self-employed if you take ownership while you are working for someone else. If you take the time to learn every facet of a business, you could be better prepared to attempt entrepreneurship or to partner with someone on a business venture. Accountability also breeds respect.

Ask questions, do not assume

Asking questions can be a difficult skill to master. It is generally easier to just assume, instead of asking questions that will help you uncover the answers you may need to achieve a task. Easier is not always better though. Sometimes someone's motivations for a decision may not be based on what you assumed they were based on, and in turn this can substantially decrease your value. An example of this is if a buyer is looking to purchase a television, and a salesperson assumes that the buyer is only price shopping. The buyer may be looking for specific features and already have a budget in mind, but the salesperson shows them the least expensive television because the salesperson assumes that is what the buyer wants. The buyer then goes elsewhere and purchases a television for substantially more, and the original salesperson earns nothing. This does not apply solely to "sales", although sales skills are used in many facets of life that people do not realize. During a job interview, you are selling yourself whether you realize it or not. Asking the right questions during a job interview can help you uncover the employer's motivations. Once you know the employer's motivations, you can position yourself to build value and negotiate effectively.

Manage your time

Time management can be an essential skill towards building your personal value. Prioritizing and scheduling your time can be an asset to employers and/or yourself. Some of the most successful people you know are also some of the most effective time managers in the world. There is an entire chapter of this book dedicated to discussing time management, as this is a crucial skill to learn and master.

Evolve yourself and adapt

The work/hobbies you are doing now can, and most likely will, change over the course of ten years. Think about the world ten years ago and how different it is today. Are you doing exactly what you were doing ten years ago? The answer for many people would be no. This is where evolving yourself and adapting to the world around you are essential. Many of the most successful companies in the world are constantly evolving, sometimes on a month-to-month basis. At their core, they may be offering the same service they were offering ten years ago, but the way they market their services may be different now. If you do not adapt to the changes around you, you can substantially decrease your value by slowing your own productivity. By evolving yourself and adapting, you can increase your value because your peers may be slow to adapt and get left behind. No matter the field you are in, staying current in your knowledge, skills and expertise can offer you staying power. Additionally, evolving yourself can keep you employed if something drastic changes in your industry.

There have been "hot jobs" in the past. In you are in a trendy field currently, and the work you are doing now becomes obsolete in five years, you could be unemployed for a while if you have not evolved yourself. This is where having a strong resume and building your personal value can help you earn. If you have built a good reputation for yourself, you may be able to find employment quickly by utilizing your skills and translating those skills into a different position. This also applies if you are self-employed, depending on what you do for work. If the goods or services you are currently selling are no longer in demand, it may be time to do something different. Whether that means closing shop, reinventing your company, or just working for someone else, the choice is yours at that point. If you do not evolve yourself and adapt however, you may substantially reduce your long-term earnings and cripple yourself financially over time.

The skills and activities that were covered in this chapter are meaningful ways to build your personal value. Your value will determine what you are worth. When you are worth more, you can then earn more per hour you spend working. In future chapters, we will examine how increased earnings can benefit you financially throughout your lifetime. Once you have increased your personal value, you can then begin to use that equity to invest in yourself.

Chapter Checklist

In this chapter we discussed specific skills and activities that can help increase your personal value. Are you doing the following consistently to help increase your personal value?

- Do you honestly believe in yourself?
- Are you open-minded (flexible)?
- Are you acquiring skills?
- Are you setting goals?
- Are you communicating effectively?
- Are you building a strong resume?
- Are you earning accolades?
- Are you utilizing your planning ability?
- Are you collaborating with anyone?
- Are you building your network?
- Are you taking care of yourself?
- Have you learned to negotiate?
- Are you negotiating effectively?
- Do you take ownership (accountability)?
- Are you asking questions instead of assuming?
- Are you evolving yourself and adapting?

Are you doing most of/all these things consistently? If you are inconsistent in your behaviors and mannerisms, it can be difficult to maintain any personal value you have built for yourself.

V. Investing in Yourself

Throughout the course of your life, you will probably hear the phrase "invest in yourself" at least a few times. It sounds great and it sounds smart, but what does it really mean to invest in yourself? The phrase itself is subjective and may have completely different meanings depending on who you speak to about the phrase. The goal of this chapter is to define what investing in yourself could mean to you, and for you to be able take the information in this chapter and apply it to your current circumstances. Again, keep in mind that the phrase "invest in yourself" is subjective, so there could be countless other ways for you to invest in yourself beyond what is listed here. We will start with some basic concepts in this chapter. You can then take these concepts, learn from them, and continue to find additional ways to invest in yourself to the point where other people will want to invest in you.

Education

Some of the ways to invest in yourself may not cost you actual money. You can obtain a public-school education for free just about anywhere in America, as well as many other places in the world. You do have to invest your time, and hopefully by now you are starting to see that your time is valuable. You can also become successful while being "uneducated" in the traditional sense of not finishing high school, college etc., if you choose to. There are many examples of people who did not finish school and went on to achieve great things. However, they still obtained an "education". They just educated themselves in different ways and increased their value to the point where other people were willing to invest their time/money into that person. Regardless, using education to invest in yourself speaks to topics we have discussed in previous chapters about building your personal value. When you educate yourself, you can begin to acquire skills that are valuable in the workplace. Once you have acquired skills, your knowledge in the skills you have obtained can be translated into money via a job or the ability to be self-employed. The topic of being employed vs. being self-employed is a topic that will be discussed later as well.

Take notes and be organized

This may seem like basic advice, but this is possibly the most powerful way to invest in yourself. Depending on your field of work and your role, you could be presented with new information at a fast pace and in a variety of ways every day. What you do with that information can shape who you are as a person and how people view you. This is especially prudent for anyone who is currently in a leadership role (or plans to be) and/or entrepreneurs. If you think of a groundbreaking idea/concept at any time but forget to take note of it, that's valuable information that just goes to waste. You cannot expand on the idea because you forgot about it. Also, if you are in any kind of role where people rely on you and you forget to accomplish an important task because it was not noted anywhere, that can decrease your value as well. Some successful people need assistants and other handlers to help them stay organized. If you are the only one in charge though, or your own boss, being disorganized can devalue you or completely derail any success you are attempting to build upon.

Create, and build awareness in your personal brand

Consuming endless amounts of content on social media, without having a personal brand, can be a tremendous waste of time. Whether you realize it or not, your name is your personal brand. The content you produce on social media is the world's impression of you, so do not take this for granted. In today's world, there are multiple social media platforms that allow you to authentically express yourself. If you successfully create a personal brand, that could be the springboard for many opportunities for you. Your personal brand could raise awareness about who you are as a person and can help you build relationships. Your personal brand can also benefit you in the workplace. Once you are educated in a field of employment, you can build awareness with other people about your knowledge in that field through your personal brand. If you choose to not have a network of people around you that know who you are and what you can do, you can severely limit your earnings potential or your ability to advance within your field. This is where investing in yourself becomes a vital part of maximizing your earnings, while minimizing the time you need to spend working. Many companies that you deem to be successful have a high level of brand awareness, which means you personally know their name brand and what they represent. As a person, you can brand yourself and build awareness in your personal brand. In many situations in recent years, someone's personal brand is one of the most powerful drivers of their business ventures. Building awareness in your brand may not cost you actual money. There is a time commitment involved, and you will have to decide whether you choose to commit the valuable resource of time to build your personal brand or not. If you plan on being employed by others for the rest of your career though, having a personal brand can be the difference between receiving job offers or not.

Networking

Without a strong network you can limit your earnings potential. Once you have defined who you are as a person and you have started to build your personal brand, your network can help you spread knowledge about your brand. When you build strong relationships in the workforce or on social media (regardless of the industry) there will be more opportunities for you to expand your knowledge, skills and possibly earnings potential. Also keep in mind that if you are open-minded (flexible), you may find opportunities within other industries to apply your skills. You may then want to take your career in a different direction altogether. By applying some of the skills and activities that were discussed earlier, networking can be one of the best ways to invest in yourself. Again, there is a time commitment involved. You may be comfortable with your earnings and the amount of time you are required to spend working in your current field of employment, and you may deem it unnecessary to network. For many people, especially people in sales (or sales-related industries), you can also do yourself a tremendous disservice by not building a strong network.

Invest actual money

The first four ways to invest in yourself in this chapter did not require real money. There are ways to spend money within each of the previous points to invest in yourself as well. In the field of education, you can choose to go to college or trade school to enhance your education on a specific topic or field. Depending on what industry you choose to enter, you can spend money on advertising to build your company or personal brand. You can even choose to spend money on apps to help you take better notes. With regards to networking, you can spend money to barter deals with other influential people to help increase your network. Or perhaps you choose to apply all the skills you have learned and open your own business, which will almost certainly require a monetary investment of some sort. We are going to cover more on that in the next chapter but investing actual money to open a company can be an extremely risky proposition if you are not prepared.

Everything covered in this chapter requires a time commitment. If your goal is to maximize your earnings, the time commitment to invest in yourself can ultimately help you achieve your goal. As we discussed earlier, there may be many more ways than listed in this chapter to invest in yourself. Investing in yourself can offer you the opportunity to eventually become your own boss in some regard, or to eventually be your own boss. In the next chapter we are going to discuss how working for others vs. working for yourself can impact your earnings potential. You can then decide if the option of self-employment, or a version of self-employment, is an option that can benefit you both personally and professionally.

Chapter Checklist

In this chapter we discussed a few examples of ways to invest in yourself. Are you doing the following to invest in your own self-worth?

- Are you educating yourself via the education system or some other version of a learning academy? This includes certifications, work courses or anything else to increase your knowledge base.
- Do you take notes so you can remember whatever is most important to you? This is as simple as writing notes in the Notes/Scratchpad app in your smartphone.
- Are you building awareness in your personal brand? Remember, your name is your brand. The more people know about you, the more opportunities may be available to you.
- Are you networking? If not, you could potentially be missing out on valuable information and/or opportunities for yourself.
- Are you ready to spend actual money on yourself? This can have many meanings, from buying new clothes to look more professional, to spending money to start a company. The choice is yours, but timing is everything.

VI. Your Employment Options

There is no right or wrong answer when it comes to the decision of being someone's employee vs. becoming self-employed. This is a personal decision that you must make based on your own circumstances. The decision should be a well-thought-out decision though and is a decision that should never be taken lightly. There are millions of people who have tried to become entrepreneurs and failed for a variety of reasons. Even though working for yourself can allow you the ability to earn more, it is not an absolute certainty that working for yourself will help you earn more money during your lifetime. There are a multitude of factors to consider when making the decision to be employed by others vs. working for yourself, plus the time commitment involved in either decision. Opening a business and failing can take many years away from the amount of time you can earn money in your lifetime, in addition to wasting the money it took to start and run the business. Also, the decision of being employed by others vs. being self-employed does not necessarily have to be an either/or decision. There are people who go into business for themselves while working for other people and have experienced success while doing so. In this chapter, we are going to cover the difference between being employed vs. being self-employed and offer perspective to help you make the choice that you may ultimately feel is best.

The facts about being employed by others

Being employed by someone can typically be safer than going into business on your own for a variety of reasons. There may be multiple companies with job openings at any given time within your field, depending on your line of work/industry. Even if one opportunity does not work out, there could be another opportunity available to you if you decide to move on from a company. This allows you to continue earning throughout the course of your life with very few breaks in income. Here are a few pros and cons of working for other people that will be expanded upon:

Pros

Generally safer way to earn, less risk
Ability to be "off the clock" (depending on your line of work and role)
Availability of multiple opportunities means less breaks in income/earnings
The possibility of still being in the top 5% of earners in the U.S. or worldwide
Camaraderie

Cons

Usually there is a "cap" on earnings
You may never truly be "the boss"
You may be more experienced than your superior
Workplace environment could be toxic
Your job may not be safe at all, you can earn "too much" sometimes

There are plenty more positive and negative characteristics that can be listed under pros and cons, but these are the most prudent to the discussion. If you have the right workplace environment and your job is mostly secure, working for others can be a great way to earn a living. Conversely, working for others can become a nightmare depending on your level of knowledge/expertise and who you work for. The specific employment situation you are in will dictate how manageable working for others is for you, and your own personal experience will be a factor as well.

When it comes to earnings, there is a certain comfort in knowing how much you will be paid if you have a salary position. The downside is if you are not earning enough to pay your bills, your personal life can become uncomfortable. Also, there is typically a "cap" (maximum amount you will be paid) associated with your earnings when working for others. The cap could be determined by the position you are working or by your employer. Again, if you are comfortable with the cap and you are happy with what you do for work, then working for others can be a stress-free venture. There is also a possibility that you could uncomfortably exceed your cap by your employer's standards, depending on the line of work. In certain cases, exceeding your cap could put your job in jeopardy. Your employer may decide to find someone else who is willing to work within the employer's cap and move on from you. Only you can decide what you are comfortable with, regarding your earnings and your mental health, while working for others.

When it comes to the time aspect associated with working for others, you can potentially achieve a comfortable work/home life balance for yourself. Typically working for other people allows you to leave your work in your office when you leave your job for the day (meaning you do not have to stress about it during your personal time). This is not always the case, and sometimes that can have more to do with you personally than your employer. The downside is that there are many toxic workplace environments and cultures that can make showing up for work an exhausting exercise. There are also plenty of workplace environments where camaraderie and collaboration are paramount, and the workplace can be extremely rewarding both personally and professionally. The owner of the business, or your direct superior, can also play a major role in your decision. If you work for an owner or boss who is open-minded and enjoys collaborative thinking, you could find yourself feeling as though you are working for yourself (in a way) while earning a safe paycheck. On the opposite side of this, if you are working for an owner or a boss who is unqualified for their position, you may feel as though you do not have a voice in the company. That can become frustrating to the point that you may want to move on from that employer.

The choice is ultimately yours when it comes to deciding if working for others is right for you. If you are thinking about becoming self-employed, typically a best practice is to work for someone else in your line of work and earn as much as possible, while learning about the field you are in. You may find that after being in a certain line of work for some time, it is not what you thought it would be. It is then safer to go work for someone else and learn a new field before attempting to open a business. As stated earlier, the decision to start your own business is not a decision to be taken lightly. We will discuss the pros and cons of becoming self-employed next.

The facts about becoming and being self-employed

Being self-employed can be rewarding and frustrating. It can be stress-free or exhausting. It can be great for you and has the potential to ruin you. There tends to be more extremes when working for yourself because there is typically more risk involved with being self-employed. A lot of people like to look at only the positives when they think about being self-employed and ignore the negatives. That has worked out for some people, while crippling others financially. There are a substantial number of factors to consider before attempting to become self-employed. If done properly, the rewards can be life altering. If you ignore the risks though, the results could be disastrous. We will first examine what is required to start your own business, before we discuss the pros and cons.

Before you get started

When examining the decision to become self-employed, the business you are planning to start will dictate how much capital is required to start the business. Also, a best practice is to examine your personal situation before even thinking about starting a business. It could take months or sometimes years to start turning a profit. Do you have enough money in your personal bank account to support yourself, your family, and the business until it turns a profit? Another factor that many people do not consider before becoming self-employed is that the business you open could require you to continuously invest back into the business. Just because a business is turning a profit, does not mean that you can put the entire profit back into your personal bank account. If your business expands and cannot afford its own bills, that will eventually catch up to itself and start draining your personal bank account. People also tend to forget that you still need to pay taxes when you are self-employed. Not preparing to pay taxes may hurt you financially but could also potentially land you in jail if you do not pay your taxes. These are just a few factors you may need to consider prior to starting your own business.

When examining the pros and cons, there again tends to be higher highs and lower lows. We will examine a few of the pros and cons of being self-employed, then we will expand on each:

Pros

The possibility of unlimited earnings potential
You are the decision maker and decide your own fate
The time commitment could be less than working for others
Personal gratification

Cons

You could earn less than working for other people, or nothing at all
You are the decision maker and decide your own fate
The time commitment could be far greater than being employed by others
Potential for greater exposure to legal action

The list of pros and cons could be far longer. We will focus on the main reasons why people become self-employed, and why many people may not necessarily find the success they were hoping for. From an earnings perspective, one of the main reasons people become self-employed is because they believe they can earn more than working for others. That is potentially true, but there is a large percentage of entrepreneurs that make the same or less than if they were to work for someone else. The amount of money you will be able to transfer from your business bank account to your personal bank account will depend on the success of the business. There are some businesses that are very capital dependent. A business may generate high sales volume, however, that does not mean that you are going to see that income reflected in your personal bank account. There are some businesses that require hundreds of thousands of dollars to operate every month, that do not turn a profit. The owner of that business may pay themselves a salary every month from the business, but that salary might be less than working for someone else using the same skills they are using to run their own business. This is just a realistic perspective about the income you could generate by being self-employed. What we are going to discuss next is the time is takes to be self-employed, and how that relates to The Business of Time.

Becoming self-employed can also help you achieve what has been discussed many times throughout this book, which is to earn more while working less. Being self-employed is not the only way to achieve this, and there are many other factors to consider. The option of self-employment could be the start of your journey though. You can still earn more while working less as you work for others, so hopefully that is not the only driving factor as you decide which option is right for you. Working for yourself just might make earning more while working less an easier task, if done properly. There are some basic principles that were discussed earlier in this book that I encourage you to read again about building your personal value. Just because you think you have a great idea, does not mean that the world thinks your idea is great. Or that the idea has not already been thought about and presented/tried and failed. Or that you have the means or capital to advance your idea. So be cautious about trying your hand at becoming self-employed. Please do your research before you decide to dive in, head-first. You might find that the time commitment just to weigh all the factors involved with becoming self-employed can be daunting and discouraging. Then you may know that being self-employed is just not right for you, personally.

All of this is just to caution you before you attempt to become self-employed. The goal is simply to offer a realistic perspective before you make the decision, because becoming self-employed is a decision that could occupy a lot of your time. If you make a poorly planned attempt at being self-employed, that could be counterproductive towards achieving your goal of earning more while working less.

At this point, we have discussed being employed vs. becoming self-employed at length. Now we will discuss a balance of being both employed by others and being self-employed at the same time.

Being self-employed while working for others

You could achieve a happy medium, and more income, if you decide to become self-employed and work for others at the same time. This is a concept that is often not thought about by the average working individual. There are plenty of ways to earn income for yourself, while you have a job working for someone else. We will discuss a few of the pros and cons before we discuss the subject further.

Pros
More income
Possibility of learning more skills
Different mentality about work (ownership)
Safety and security

Cons
Time commitment could be overwhelming
No guarantee of additional earnings
Possibility that you could earn more just working for a different employer
Lost wages/money if self-employment does not work

As you can see, there is still more risk involved with this strategy than just working for someone else. The reality of being self-employed is that it is not as glamorous as most people think unless you succeed. Conversely, if you succeed, the reward can be gratifying on both a personal and professional level. With that being said, we will discuss the pros and cons a bit more.

On the income side, being self-employed while working for others can help you grow financially. It also depends on what you choose to do while being self-employed. If the business you choose requires a heavy financial investment, you may have to prepare yourself to make a time commitment to that investment. You may have to quit your steady job, and focus your efforts on the investment you made, to avoid a potential loss altogether if something goes wrong. If what you are doing to be self-employed can manage itself and earn you money without a major time commitment, that will be helpful to your earnings. Also, depending on the time commitment and your level of knowledge and skills, you may just earn more money by finding one high-paying job instead of trying to juggle both.

On the time side, working for other people while trying to be self-employed can be an exhausting venture. Depending on what you choose to do, and the time commitment involved to make it successful, you could spend every hour of your day working whether you would like to or not. Again, if what you choose does not require a massive time commitment, this route could be rewarding. You will need to choose carefully though and again decide if you are prepared to lose time with friends and family to achieve your financial goals. To some people, although this could be financially beneficial, the loss in personal time is not worth the earnings.

The purpose of this chapter was to provide you with some perspective, and perhaps open your eyes to possibilities that you may not have previously thought of. A best practice is to research the different ways of becoming self-employed, to see if something sparks your interest. You may be surprised at all the different ways you can earn money, while still working a steady job. Many people view working for someone or being self-employed as an either-or type of decision, but it does not have to be. The key is to find the right balance for yourself. The decision should ultimately be based on what you are comfortable with, and what makes you feel satisfied. Once you make the determination of the employment option(s) that work(s) best for you, the next step is to maximize your earnings.

Chapter Checklist

In this chapter we discussed the decision of being employed by others vs. being self-employed. Which one (or both) is right for you?

- Have you thought about and thoroughly examined this decision yet?
- Do you have a good paying, secure job?
- Are you comfortable in your current earnings?
- Are you saving money from your job earnings?
- How are you trending towards retirement? At what age will you be able to retire and live comfortably?
- What are you passionate about? Can your passion translate into a career choice?
- If you choose to become self-employed, how will you make money?
- If you are opening a business, what will your expenses be monthly?
- Can you survive for a few months while your startup business is not profitable?
- Do you have time to have a job while starting a business to earn income?
- Are you prepared for the time commitment?
- Will this make you happy?

VII. Maximizing Your Earnings

Regardless of whether you choose to be employed by others or be self-employed (or a combination of both), the key to earning more while working less is to maximize your earnings. In previous chapters, we discussed skills and activities that can help you maximize your earnings. In this chapter, we will discuss additional steps that you can take to help you maximize your earnings. The following bullet points are tips to help you earn more, in conjunction with the skills and activities you have read about previously.

1. Examine yourself as a person

   The first step towards maximizing your earnings is to understand yourself as a person. Some people are great public speakers, while others are great strategic thinkers. Some people can do both while others can do neither, but the others still possess skills and value. You need to be brutally honest with yourself and think about what you can do, and what you are willing to do (your choice), to earn for yourself. Also, determine how many hours you are willing to work to achieve your financial goals. Some people have no problem working most of their day while others would prefer to work very few hours in a day, even if it means lost wages. Once you have determined who you are, what you can do, and what you are comfortable with, you can then begin to look at your options to earn. By doing so, you will have a clearer picture of ways to earn for yourself while maintaining your happiness.

2. Establish your personal brand to enhance your value

   Establishing a personal brand has been discussed repeatedly throughout this book. The reason is because your personal brand can build awareness about who you are as an individual, which can help you maximize your personal value. As discussed in previous chapters, acquiring skills and earning accolades is important. However, it can still be difficult to find employment if you acquire skills/earn accolades without networking. The relationships you build through your personal brand can make you more valuable as a person and provide you with additional earning opportunities. You can then make an educated decision about your employment options, from a position of strength, based on all the avenues available to you to earn money.

3. Evaluate your employment options

   Once you know who you are and what you can/will do, the next step is to evaluate what options are available for you to earn a living. For most people, if they evaluate themselves and their personal skills, then take the time to research what they could be doing to earn, they will uncover many options to earn for themselves that they may not have originally thought about. For example, if you are a skilled administrative professional, your skills translate to most office environments. If you ever lose your job, you may be able to easily replace that job because your skills are transferable. Those same skills can also be utilized to become self-employed as an independent contractor. You can then be hired on a contract basis to help companies become more organized, while setting your own schedule. There is more security in working for others on a full-time basis, but more flexibility if you choose to become a self-employed, independent contractor. You have options, and the choice is yours.

4. The option of self-employment

   Self-employment can be a risky proposition, as previously discussed throughout this book. It can also be rewarding from both a financial, and mental health, standpoint. The key to exercising this option is timing. As rare as it may be, there are some people who are ready to be self-employed straight out of high school or possibly even beforehand. They have enough capital, limited responsibilities, have established a personal brand, and have enough value to market themselves and be successful. For others, and depending on the industry they have chosen, it could take years to be at the point where they have acquired enough skills/capital to open their own business. Again, you should be honest with yourself before you make the decision to become self-employed. You can keep the option open for yourself though, even if it is nothing more than a goal to work towards. You may also decide that being self-employed is just not right for you, because being self-employed is not for everyone. When you have carefully considered the option of self-employment though, you have at least contemplated multiple options to maximize your earnings.

5. Negotiate to earn what you deserve

   The final step to maximizing your earnings, once you have established your value, is to negotiate for additional earnings. You should not accept a monetary offer for yourself that is substantially lower than your market/industry value, just because it is barely acceptable to you. There may be certain times in life when you need a job, and you are willing to accept any offer just to pay your bills. Let that be a short-term solution though, until you can find a job that aligns with your actual market value. The reason is because you can hurt yourself financially over time, and that can have a major impact on your road to retirement. Here are a few examples of lost wages over time:

   A. *You accept $50,000 in annual wages as opposed to $60,000 or $70,000 per year*
      Your lost wages calculated, long-term:
      $10,000 additional per year * 30 years =
      $300,000 in lost wages
      $20,000 additional per year * 30 years =
      $600,000 in lost wages

B. *You are selling a good or service at a lower amount than a competitor*
Your lost wages calculated, long-term:
Your company sells product A for $5.
Your competitor is selling the same product for $10.
$5 in additional profit per unit * 100 units sold = *$500 per month in lost earnings*
$5 in additional profit per unit * 1,200 annual units = *$6,000 annual lost earnings*
$6,000 in annual lost earnings * 30 years = ***$180,000 lost earnings***

When examining lost wages from a long-term perspective, you can see how not earning every dollar possible can affect your ability to retire. This works in both the short-term and long-term, but the difference can be extreme long-term. Here is something else to consider: earning more at your main employer might mean that you do not have to work a second job or work overtime, which allows you to have more personal time. Do not be afraid to negotiate for what you feel is fair and what you feel your maximum value is. If you are afraid to negotiate, you may need to learn how to overcome your fear, because negotiation can help you avoid lost wages over time. By doing so, you give yourself options that you may not have previously had before. These options include retiring earlier than originally planned, or potentially just working less and affording yourself more personal time.

Chapter Checklist

In this chapter we discussed how to maximize your earnings. Are you doing the following to earn as much as possible?

- Are you honest with yourself? If you inflate your own personal value, or you tend to lower your own value, it can be hard to truly maximize your earnings. Sometimes an objective opinion from someone else can be helpful when evaluating your self-worth.
- Do you have a personal brand on social media? If not, do you at least have a solid reputation in your industry to substantiate your value?
- Have you evaluated every earning option available to you?
- Have you given serious thought to the option of self-employment? If you have not, why not?
- Do you feel as though you are earning fair or adequate value? Are you at peace with your overall earnings, or do you want more?
- Are you attempting to negotiate for what you feel are fair earnings? Or do you just accept any offer that is presented to you?
- Have you considered the impact lost wages/earnings can have over time?

VIII. Managing Your Time

Effectively managing your time can help you substantially reduce stress in your life. For many people, poor time management is the root cause of why they may feel overwhelmed on any given day. Managing your time efficiently can be the missing link between earning a good income and a feeling of general satisfaction/happiness in your life. Also, effective time management can help you to find additional time in your day. You can use the additional time to either find ways to earn more for yourself, or just take the additional time to do the things that you enjoy most. The following are ways to help you better manage your time, so you can reap the benefits of the additional time available to you.

Prioritize Your Time

It is easy to get lost in life and to not pay attention to what you deem most important. Emergencies happen, distractions occur, and sometimes you may have a tremendous amount of information presented to you at any given moment. Any of these situations can be overwhelming, even if you are already good at managing your time. The key to managing your time effectively is to be able to identify what you *need* to do, then place the tasks you need to accomplish in an order of what is most important to you. A best practice is to create a list of tasks that you need to accomplish, then numerically order those tasks by level of importance. If you take care of the tasks that can cause the most stress in your life, you can help yourself from feeling overwhelmed. You can then move on to the less important tasks in your life, knowing you have accomplished the most necessary tasks first. Once you know how to prioritize what is important to you, you can then work on *when* you want to accomplish the tasks that need to be handled.

Scheduling Your Time

Scheduling your time can be an invaluable skill. If you do not schedule your time, you may agree to do too much with the time that you have available. This can lead to stress and may affect both your personal and professional life. In your personal life, you could agree to spend your weekends in multiple places and forget that you have yourself booked to be two places at once. You may then disappoint whoever you were planning on meeting with by cancelling at the last minute or just not showing up. This could increase your stress level, especially if you deemed both meetings to be important on some level. In your professional life, you may miss a deadline or forget to attend a meeting if you are not scheduling your time. This could be a negative reflection on you, which can (and most likely will) decrease your personal value. If you decrease your value, you could lose wages/earnings over time. You may not earn a better raise or a promotion. You could also be terminated, because your boss may deem your salary to not be worth the aggravation it causes them. Any of these situations can increase your stress level. This concept also (and, especially) applies if you choose to be self-employed. If you schedule meetings and forget to show up, your clients may choose to pay you less or not pay you at all. If you earn a reputation as being unreliable, you may not be a client's first choice when they need a service. This could be especially damaging to your income, as reviews are a very prevalent part of the general public's decision making in today's world.

Dictate Your Schedule

Once you have determined what you need to do and when you need to do it, you can then begin to dictate (take control of) your schedule. What this means is you can tell people when you are and are not available. You may not be comfortable with this notion yet, especially if you are the type of person that does not like to say "no" to people. However, the alternative could be that you overschedule yourself and end up over-promising and under-delivering. This could lead to disappointment in both your personal/professional life and again, increase your stress level. Once you reach a certain level of responsibility in your life, dictating your schedule could become a necessity if you would like to avoid feeling overwhelmed.

Decide between work and personal time

If you have mastered the first three concepts in this chapter, it can then become easier to decide how you choose to spend your time. For some people, they may decide that they want to work often and earn as much as possible during a span of time, then be able to relax later in life. For some people, they may not mind working at all and will have no problem working into the later years of their life. The decision most likely comes down to how much you enjoy doing what you do for work. If you would like to retire sooner, prioritize spending your time earning while maximizing your personal value/income. If you choose to spend more time doing things that you enjoy, it is still a good idea to maximize your earnings but to also be at peace with your decision to not earn as much. Regardless, you always have a choice. You may not feel as though you have a choice sometimes, depending on your financial situation. You do have the ability to choose how to spend your time though, and time management can help you examine what options are available to you with regards to earning more income.

In a later chapter of this book, we will discuss earning passive and residual income. There are many ways to earn money without having to physically work, "on-the-clock", for an employer. If you earn enough passive and residual income to support your family and retire, you could spend the majority of your time doing things that you enjoy as opposed to being forced to physically work to support your family. You may not have thought about this option yet, but this is one of the main principles of The Business of Time.

The overall theme of this chapter is that time management can be crucial to obtaining your ideal work/home life balance. If you have earned a great reputation, have reached a certain level of success in your career, and still feel unsatisfied, time management could be the missing piece to help you feel satisfied/happy. In the next few chapters, we are going to further expand on actual methods and tactics to market and sell yourself to help you achieve your maximum value. When you are able to earn as much as possible during your working hours, you can then manage your time better and give yourself the ability to work as much or as little as you *choose* to.

Chapter Checklist

In this chapter we discussed ways to manage your time. Are you doing the following to get the most out of your time?

- Do you prioritize what is most important? By prioritizing your time, you can feel a greater sense of accomplishment by completing what matters most to you.
- Are you using a calendar app or some version of a calendar to schedule your time? By doing so, you can help keep yourself on track and avoid stressful situations due to overbooking your time.
- Are you able to dictate your own time, or are other people dictating your schedule? If other people are dictating your schedule, that can lead to stress and unhappiness, unless you have specifically appointed someone to manage your time for you.
- Have you researched any ways to earn passive or residual income? If not, this will be covered in a later chapter of this book.
- Do you feel happy or satisfied with your life? If you are not satisfied, could managing your time help to change your feelings?

IX. What is your time worth?

Before you begin any type of negotiation, a best practice would be to identify how much your time is worth. In theory, if your value is high you should be able to charge more for your services. From a practical standpoint though, you may find this challenging. There are many reasons for this, and there are a few checkpoints you should consider (in addition to what you have read thus far) before you attempt to cash in on the investments you have made in yourself. Once you have checked all the boxes though, you may be ready to ask to be paid your maximum value and begin to earn what you deserve.

Fundamentally, the ability to earn what you are worth starts with the belief that you are worth what you will be asking others to pay you. The reason this is important is because you will most likely have to sell someone (or many people) on the idea of paying you what you believe you are worth. When you attempt to sell someone on an idea and you lack confidence, you also lack the conviction that is required for someone else to believe you are worth the money you are asking for. This applies to both working for others and being self-employed. Before you attempt to sell yourself, you should have a solid foundation. Here are a few examples of things you can do to build a solid foundation for yourself:

1. You have a unique skill or an idea that is groundbreaking. Your idea/process must better than already existing businesses in the market.
2. You have substantial experience in a field, and you combine your experience with work ethic.
3. You have tangible evidence (degrees, certificates, statistics, references, etc.) as proof that you have obtained the skills required to complete the job/task at-hand.
4. You have written a business plan, and possibly a marketing plan, if you are looking for someone to invest in you or a startup business.

If you have a solid foundation, this makes it easier to believe in yourself. Believing in yourself is the first step towards being able to sell someone on your worth.

In addition to believing in yourself, you should also educate yourself on the market for your services. This will provide you with additional confidence and will also help you determine if your asking price is fair. A few questions you should research before you attempt to sell yourself include:

1. Who can you sell to? (employers or potential customers for your business/services)
2. How large is the market (or how many candidates are applying for a position)?
3. How much competition exists in the market?
4. Do you offer something unique or better than your competition?
5. What is the average price for the product/service you are offering or the average salary for the position you are applying for?

6. If you are going to ask for more than the average, *why* are you (or your product/service) worth more than your competition?
7. Do you need money now or can you wait for someone to pay you what you are worth?
8. Are you willing to negotiate?

Once you have answered these questions, you should be able to confidently sell your value because you know what the market is for your services. The answers to these questions can also help you determine a fair market value for yourself/your services. If you have maximized your personal value, asking for what you are worth just becomes a natural progression and the next step.

Below is an equation to help calculate your hourly rate. A simple way to calculate a value for your services is to take the amount of money you would like to make annually, then divide that into an hourly rate. Here is a simple example of the equation to calculate the hourly rate you would like to charge:

Annual goal = $208,000 annual earnings
Annual goal divided by weeks in the year =
$208,000/52 weeks = $4,000/week
$4,000/week divided by 40 hours in the work week is your hourly rate
$4,000/week divided by a 40-hour work week =
$100/hour

This is a simple example. This math equation can be edited to fit your lifestyle. If you would like to work half of the time, but make the same money, you can increase your hourly rate. Example:

Annual goal = $208,000 annual earnings
Annual goal divided by weeks in the year =
$208,000/52 weeks = $4,000/week
$4,000/week divided by 20 hours in the work week is your hourly rate
$4,000/week divided by a 20-hour work week =
$200/hour

The same math equation works even if you do not want/need to make $200,000+ annually. You might be working for someone else currently, you dislike your job, and would like to become self-employed. If you are earning good money, but you are unsure of how to replace your income, the same equation can potentially help to ease your concerns. You can then begin your journey to entrepreneurship.

Annual goal = $72,800 annual earnings
Annual goal divided by weeks in the year = $72,800/52 weeks = $1,400/week
$1,400/week divided by 40 hours in the work week is your hourly rate
$1,400/week divided by a 40-hour work week =
$35/hour

The reason this last equation is discussed is because if you examine the $100/hour equation ($100 per hour * 40-hour work week * 52 weeks in a year = $208,000), you may think it is easy to earn $208,000 annually. For some people, it is. Keep this in mind though: $208,000 would put you in the top 10% of American earners. Do not overinflate your asking price simply because this is what you *wish* to earn.

If you have not yet acquired the skills, or you are not currently working in a position where $100 per hour is standard earnings, you should not be charging $100 per hour for your services. If you plan on charging $100 per hour for clerical services (such as filing and answering phones) when many clerical professionals earn anywhere between $15-$20 per hour (or less), you may struggle to find work because your asking price is too high. Even if you are the best at what you do, you might be hard-pressed to find a business owner willing to pay 5x (times) the going rate for the same service when there are hundreds of clerical professionals looking for jobs every day. It is imperative that you match your skills/services to the market value so you can consistently find enough work to earn your annual goal. Asking $100 per hour for clerical services is a lofty goal, however if you can only find 5 hours of work per week this is what your annual earnings would be:

$100 per hour * 5 hours per week = $500/week.
$500/week * 52 weeks = $26,000 annually

This equation might work for some people but as previously stated, it will be difficult to retire comfortably if you are only earning $26,000 annually over the course of 30+ years (especially if you have children). Answering the 8 questions posed earlier in this chapter will help you to avoid the pitfall of setting your asking price too high. This is especially prudent if you are self-employed. As an entrepreneur, you can dictate how much you will charge for your services, but you are also responsible for filling your calendar with a consistent 40-hour work week. Once you have determined an appropriate value for your services, the next steps will be to market yourself and sell yourself to earn the amount that you believe you deserve.

Chapter Checklist

In this chapter we discussed the value/worth of your time. Have you thought about the following to accurately assess your value?

- Have you built a solid foundation for yourself? Without a solid foundation of skills and accolades, it can be hard for others to see the value in what you offer.
- Have you done proper planning? Try to assess yourself from an outsider's perspective. When people view your resume, social media profiles or business plan, what do they see? Also, ask for opinions from people that you trust will give you an objective view. Presentation matters to employers/potential clients.
- Have you educated yourself on the market? By knowing how much your skills or services are worth, you can avoid being rejected because you are asking for an amount that is substantially higher than the market value.
- Have you calculated what you would like to earn annually? This will help you determine if you are utilizing your skills properly. This may also help you determine if you should continue working for others, or attempt self-employment, to achieve what you feel you deserve.

X. Marketing Yourself

You know how to build your personal value now. You have learned how to equate what you want to earn annually into an hourly rate. You have also learned how to establish a fair market value for yourself. Now it is time to put it all together, test the marketplace, and earn what you believe you are worth.

In many companies, especially large-scale companies, a company will typically have both a marketing department and a sales department. The marketing department is responsible for advertising the company, the sales department is responsible for selling the company's products/services so the business can earn a profit. Whether you work for others or are self-employed, the concept of marketing yourself and selling yourself apply to your everyday life.

The main function of the marketing department in many companies is to generate leads (sales opportunities) for the sales department. When you are marketing yourself, you are attempting to generate leads for yourself. You can generate leads in many ways, depending on whether you are self-employed or employed by others.

If you are employed by others, an example of a lead could be a job opportunity you receive through a referral from a friend or family member. You may have earned the job opportunity through your social media presence, which is why personal branding is discussed at length in this book.

If you are self-employed, an example of a lead is an inquiry about your services through either your social media profiles or your website. You can then contact the person inquiring about your product(s)/services and attempt to sell them whatever it is that you offer.

The goal for many marketing departments is to generate as many leads as possible, while spending as little money as possible to generate leads. When you are marketing yourself the same concept applies, even as a job seeker. If you have not done a good job of marketing yourself as a job seeker, you are limited to the amount of job opportunities you can find via career websites. If your resume is not as impressive as other job seekers, you can be out of work for an extended period. During that period, you could be losing a substantial amount of earnings and hurt yourself financially. However, if you have a personal brand on social media, that can set you apart from other qualified candidates. The personal brand may cost you nothing, yet you could receive job opportunities that were not made readily available on career websites because an employer sought you out specifically.

If you are self-employed, the concept of generating as many leads as possible for the least amount of money spent is especially prudent. Regardless if you have a large-scale company, or are an independent contractor just looking for consulting gigs, you will need sales opportunities. The more sales opportunities you can create for free, the less you will have to spend to generate leads. You can effectively generate leads via social media, without having to spend money, through your personal brand.

A few examples of ways to market yourself through your personal brand on social media include:

1. Building a brand/business page on social media
2. Email collection/email marketing
3. Joining social media groups where you can interact with customers for your business
4. Specifically advertising your business or a promotion on social media (paid or otherwise)
5. Building a following on social media
6. Utilizing influencers to help advertise you/your product or service

These examples speak more specifically to someone who is self-employed (or businesses) vs. people who are employed by others, or job seekers. If you are employed by others, or are a job seeker, here are a few examples of how marketing yourself through your personal brand can benefit you:

1. In a sales role, you can create sales opportunities for yourself by advertising where you work and what you sell on social media.
2. If you work for a company in a non-sales role but you attract clients to the company through your social media presence, that can increase your personal value.
3. If you are a job seeker that has a following on social media, you could be deemed a person of influence by an employer. If you can bring attention to a company through your social media presence, you may be deemed more valuable than another qualified candidate.

These are just a few examples of how your personal brand can benefit you on social media. There are other ways to market yourself beyond social media as well. You can create a website for yourself/your company, although this will typically require a monetary investment. You can attend networking events/career workshops. As a business owner, you can (and possibly will have to) pay to advertise your company to help scale the business. When you are marketing yourself, just remember that the goal is to generate as many leads (sales opportunities) as possible for as little money spent as possible.

Everything said in this chapter is meant to educate you about how to increase your visibility in the workplace/marketplace. By increasing your visibility, you create awareness about who you are as an individual and what you are capable of. When you have more visibility, it is easier to create leads (sales opportunities) for yourself. When you have more leads, it becomes easier for you to make better choices and negotiate for your maximum value.

In the next chapter we will discuss how to sell yourself. Selling yourself is another step towards earning your maximum value when communicating with employer/consumers. Many large-scale companies have a sales process, which helps them maximize the amount of sales they can make on the leads they have available. You will learn a basic sales process in the next chapter, which can help you maximize the amount of money you can earn per hour/annually. This will help you to work as much or as little as you *choose* to, provided you are not living beyond your means.

Chapter Checklist

In this chapter we discussed marketing yourself to increase awareness about yourself and raise your value. Are you doing the following to build awareness about who you are and what you do?

- Are you generating enough leads (sales opportunities) for you to make good decisions? This concept applies whether you work for others, are a job seeker, or are self-employed.
- Have you created at least one social media profile for yourself? You can start advertising yourself through social media, without having to spend money to gain visibility.
- Have you investigated all social media platforms available to you? You do not need to be on every platform, but you should be on the platforms that best fit your personality.
- Should you have a personal or business website? If you own a business, you should have a website. Personal websites are more specific to you as an individual. For many people, a personal website is unnecessary. If your company is built around your personal name though, you should have a website to increase awareness about your brand.

XI. Selling yourself

This chapter will explain how selling yourself can help you capitalize on the value you have built for yourself, then maximize the money you earn. Sales is an integral part of life, whether you realize it or not. Almost every business relies on sales to survive, and your ability to sell yourself is a crucial skill that will benefit you for as many years as you are working. This is true whether you are self-employed or work for others. If you work for others, the ability to sell yourself will help you earn a higher paying job, or a raise at your current employer. If you are self-employed, the ability to sell yourself and/or your company's products/services is essential to your survival. You may have the best product available, but it can be difficult to maintain profits if you cannot articulate your product's value and earn the amount of money you are asking for your product via sales.

The more you can earn per transaction, self-employed or otherwise, the more ability you will have to choose what you would like to do in life. You can choose to work less, or you can choose to work as much as you would like, and potentially set yourself up for retirement sooner.

In previous chapters, negotiation has been mentioned numerous times as an essential skill in life. Negotiation and sales are not necessarily mutually exclusive, because there is a sales aspect to negotiation. In sales, typically a sale occurs when a consumer's perception of value meets the price. In negotiation, if the compromise of whatever is being negotiated meets the other party's perception of value, the interested party may agree to the compromise. The key to both is *value*, which is why there is an entire chapter of this book dedicated to building your personal value.

If you, as a person, are valuable (self-employed or otherwise) and people are excited to spend money for what you offer, you can be less focused on what the market is for your services. This is especially true if you offer something unique. When you offer something unique, there is sometimes not a fair comparison to what you offer. This, in turn, increases the value of what you offer. However, you still need to be able to articulate/explain what it is that you offer and build value in yourself or the product/service. This is the essence of sales, and the reason why people will pay you what you are asking for your services.

In this chapter, we will review the steps to successfully sell yourself. There may be variances in your approach depending on your situation, but the general premise of these steps should be the same whenever you are selling yourself. Each of these steps will note the differences in working for others as an employee vs. being self-employed, to help articulate how to sell yourself in either situation.

Be prepared

<u>As an employee</u>: While working for others, being prepared means to be equipped with facts when you attend any meeting. If you are going to a job interview, you should always come prepared with a resume, and

do research on the company you are applying to. In the event you are asking for a raise, you should have facts and/or tangible evidence about what your contributions are to the company you work for. Measurable statistics are powerful, and you should be prepared to present what your meaningful contributions are to a company whenever you are negotiating for a raise.

As self-employed: When you work for yourself, there are many layers to being prepared. Similar to the concept of having a resume, a best practice is to have reference materials for yourself/your business available for potential clients to research and review. Also, prior to any kind of presentation/sales pitch, you should discover as much as possible about your potential client by researching them. The more you can find out before a discovery call/meeting, the less time you will waste and the more focused and tailored your presentation/pitch can be. This increases your chances of closing any type of transaction.

Discovery (ask questions, do not assume)

As an employee: While working for others, you may have many opportunities to adjust your income to help yourself earn more. As an employee though, it is important to discover more about the person or company that will be paying your salary. Discovery is an important aspect of a job interview. If you are interviewing for two companies, it is important to know the benefits of both companies before you accept a position. If one company offers a 401K contribution match, while another company does not, that could mean a major difference in what you are able to earn long-term (more on this in the next chapter). Asking questions can show your employer that you care, while you are also obtaining valuable information for yourself. The questions you ask will depend on the employer, and it is important to be prepared and ask relevant questions during an interview or a performance review. When you are negotiating for a raise, an example of a discovery question could be "what do you believe a fair increase amount would be based on my production?" By asking this question during a performance review, you can gain insight into what your employer believes is fair before you attempt to negotiate for a raise.

As self-employed: When you are attempting to sell yourself or your product/service when you are self-employed, it is important to determine if there is a need for your services. Potential clients will allow you time for a sales pitch, however if you are constantly pitching to the wrong people you will waste a lot of time. Wasted time equals lost earnings when you work for yourself. Good discovery questions will not only show your potential client that you are interested in them, but also offer valuable information regarding if the client is a good fit for your services. Again, wasted time equals lost earnings. If you spend a tremendous amount of your time pitching for zero profit, you will be setting yourself back from an earnings perspective.

Present your value proposition and pricing

As an employee: Once you have determined that either a potential employer will be a good fit for you, or if your discovery questions have led you to believe there is potential for a raise, now it is time to present your value. This can be accomplished in a few ways. In the case of attempting to secure a job, you should come prepared with your resume but also have data and facts to support your claims. Depending on the position, it may be a smart idea to have a presentation prepared to review during an interview. If you are attempting to earn a raise, being prepared with your achievements and/or contributions to the company could be a powerful tool to help you earn a raise. Remember, the ability to articulate your value is a crucial element of sales. If you can articulate your value, you may also be able to find a different employer who is willing to pay you what you are worth if/when your current employer chooses not to.

As self-employed: Once you have done proper discovery and you have determined that you would like to move forward with a potential client, you then must articulate what it is that you/your company does and how it will benefit the client. Your presentation should be tailored to your potential client, so you can maximize the value of what you are presenting. This will also make the potential client more likely to move forward with your services, if they can afford what you are asking from a monetary perspective. As discussed previously, your pricing should be in line with the market unless you offer something unique or substantially better than your competitors.

Trial close (closing attempt)

As an employee: A trial close is an opportunity to learn if your efforts from the first three steps in this chapter were effective. In the event of a job interview, your trial close could be to ask for the job. In the event of a raise, a trial close could be a question such as “based on everything we’ve discussed, do you feel as though I deserve an increase in pay”? In life, if you do not ask, you will not receive in many situations.

As self-employed: Once you have finished your value proposition, you should always ask for the client's business (unless you have mutually determined with your potential client that the product/service is not a fit for either party). An example of a trial close at the end of a presentation could be: "Thank you for your time. Based on everything discussed today, it seems as though our service will benefit you. Would you like to move forward with our services today?" This gives the potential client the opportunity to say "yes" and gives you the ability to move forward with a sale.

Closing/follow up

As an employee: After a trial close or a closing question, many different scenarios could happen. You might earn either the raise, or the job, you were asking for. If you are interviewing for a job, it is also possible you may not get the job right away. Following up (asking the employer about the status or your job application) with an employer might impress an employer and could be the difference in you obtaining the job or not. If you ask for a raise, it is also possible you may not get a raise immediately when you first ask for one. Following up about your request for a raise may help you to earn a raise, eventually.

As self-employed: When you are selling yourself, or selling for yourself, you will not sell to 100% of the people you present to. However, a "no" today could be a "yes" in the future if you are following up with each of your potential clients. It is important to keep track of every potential client and stay in touch with them. When you are self-employed, it is your responsibility to create your own sales opportunities. Without enough opportunities, you will not sell enough to achieve your goals. Therefore, it is not only imperative to create as many opportunities for yourself as possible through marketing, but also to follow up with any potential clients in your pipeline. Every transaction (sale) is important, so following up and turning potential clients into actual clients (that pay you money) will have an absolute impact on your earnings.

These 5 steps are general guidelines for you to follow to help sell yourself. Depending on the type of business/position you are in, you may require a more complex and sophisticated sales process. I strongly recommend that you go beyond what you have read in this chapter to learn more about selling yourself/your business. What you have read in this chapter is just a starting point, but there is much more to sales than the general help listed here. You may have great intentions/excellent skills, but if you do not apply some/all the steps listed in this chapter, you may not be able to capitalize/earn money. If you are not effectively selling yourself, that could mean lost earnings/income.

A large portion of this book has been dedicated to discussing how to increase your personal value, to help you maximize your earnings during your physical working hours. The next chapter is about learning how to make money without having to physically work to earn it. This is one of the main premises of the Business of Time. If you can earn money without having to physically work, you can free up more time to spend however you see fit. Earning passive and/or residual income can also help you retire sooner. By doing so, you will have the ability to choose whether you would like to work, or just spend your time doing activities that you enjoy.

Chapter Checklist

In this chapter we discussed how to sell yourself. Are you doing the following to put yourself in the best position to earn money?

- Have you prepared for a situation that you will need to sell yourself?
- Do you have questions prepared for the type of situation in which you will need to sell? (examples: interview questions or discovery questions for a sales presentation).
- Are you able to present yourself, or your products/services, in a way that your audience can understand?
- Do you have an idea of how much you would like to charge for your products/services? Is the price point in alignment with the market?
- Do you have a closing question prepared?
- If you do not close "the sale", what is your follow up plan?
- Have you taken any additional steps to learn how to sell yourself/your company's services? The premise of sales (fulfill a need or solve a problem) is similar regardless of the industry you are in. However, the complexity of your business could require a more complex sales process for you to be effective at selling.

XII. Alternate ways to earn

As stated in the first chapter, having only one source of income for your entire life can make for a long road to retirement. Many of us were never taught alternate ways to earn money though, such as passive and/or residual income. This chapter is to enlighten you about different ways you can earn money, that you may not have previously known/thought about. Some of the ways you can earn money do not require you to physically work (on-the-clock). The money you earn through passive and/or residual sources can be your main source of income, or possibly an additional revenue stream for you.

When you have multiple revenue streams, it becomes easier to choose how you wish to spend your time. For many people, they begin to generate money through an additional revenue source while they are working for someone else. When they grow that source of income, that eventually becomes their main source of income and they do not *need* to work for someone else to maintain their lifestyle. If their job is steady and stress-free, they may choose to continue to work for their employer. It was their *choice* to remain at their job though, to generate additional income.

If you choose to only have one source of income for your entire career, you can still earn passive/residual income. You can earn this type of income by managing your retirement savings separately from your standard savings. By carefully investing your retirement savings, you can shorten the projected number of years it will take for you to retire. Having said that, it is important to educate yourself about the different types of savings and retirement accounts available to you. When you place your money into a retirement account, you may not be able to withdraw that money without a penalty. While there are benefits to certain retirement accounts, such as a 401K account with a company that offers a 401K match (explained further in this chapter), the additional money you earn could be less than the penalty to withdraw the money at some point. For many people, they may blindly follow other people's advice about investing in a 401K. A 401K is not the only way to invest your retirement earnings and may not be the best way to invest your retirement earnings, if you are not paying attention to your money once it is invested. We will discuss this further later in this chapter, but first we will discuss the many avenues available for you to earn passive and/or residual income.

There are many ways to earn passive or residual income. Passive/residual income is money that you earn while you are not "on the clock" and physically working to earn a living. You can do further research on the many ways to earn passive/residual income, but here are few examples:

1. Stock investments/401K accounts
2. Social media channels
3. Real estate/rental properties
4. Book sales
5. Production credits and royalties
6. Monthly subscription-based services
7. Referrals from other vendors

These options are just a few examples of ways to earn while you are not physically working. The reason stock investments/401K accounts are listed first is because many people invest in their company's 401K to earn a "company match" percentage. The company match percentage is defined as a percentage of money your company will match, dollar-for-dollar, when you invest in the company's 401K. This is a great way to earn additional money towards your retirement, and reduce your age to retire, *if you manage it properly*. Keep this in mind though: if you leave the company, you might not be able to withdraw your 401K savings without a penalty. You could roll the money into another retirement account, but there could still be penalties for withdrawing the money before age 60.

For many people, they choose to invest in a 401K, but they forget (or choose not to) manage their investments. This is an important aspect of 401Ks to educate yourself about. When the stock market crashes, you can lose some of (or all) your investment earnings if you are not invested in the right places. Many 401Ks allow you to manage your investments yourself. If you do, during a stock market crash you can simply sell off your investments and keep your money safe from the downturn of the stock market. There were two stock market crashes in recent memory, in 2008 and 2020. For many people, they gave up a large share of their gains and savings because they were not managing their investments. By doing so, this adds to the age in which you can retire and can hurt you and your family in a quest for long-term wealth.

You do not need to be a day trader to earn money through the stock market. However, what many people do not realize is that their 401K account may invested in stocks. It is important to investigate what happens to your money once you invest in a 401K or any type of retirement account, and if you have the option to manage your funds once you invest. If you do have the option to manage your funds, it is important to take the time to research how you would like to invest your earnings.

Here is an example of how managing your investments can benefit you, long term: If you manage to earn an average of $12,000 of retirement income from stock profits by investing your 401K savings, after 20 years you would have earned an additional $240,000 from stock profits. This does not include the percentage of money you invested in your 401K, plus your company match percentage. If in that same 20-year span you invested 3 percent of your earnings into your 401K and your company matched 3 percent, you would save a total of 6 percent of your annual earnings. If you earned $50,000 annually, that would be $3,000 per year between your 3 percent investment and the company match percentage of that investment. After 20 years, between your stock profits and your 401K savings, you would have saved a total of $300,000 on a $50,000 annual salary. This example assumes you only saved 3% of your earnings. If you manage your investments properly, the $12,000 annual average profit from stocks could also be substantially higher. This is just a realistic example of how profitable investing your retirement savings can be.

Also, you do not have to work for a company that offers a 401K to enter the stock market. There are numerous ways to enter the stock market via trading accounts, retirement accounts, (IRA) etc. There are many people who are unaware of how to invest, and the stock market is just one option. Keep this in mind though: the stock market is like gambling and there is no guarantee of a return on your investment. Be sure to do your homework and know your limitations before you enter the stock market. You can absolutely lose more than you gain in the stock market if you are not careful. It is best not to attempt this option unless you are familiar with the rules, guidelines, and laws of the stock market, and have done your homework first. The stock market can be volatile, but it can also be a tremendous vehicle to help you save for retirement. If done properly, investing in the stock market can shorten your road to retirement and/or make your road to retirement feel more comfortable.

Earning passive and/or residual income, and/or managing your retirement savings separately, can drastically shorten the amount of time you need to spend physically working. If you are not doing either though, you could be setting yourself up to work until your later years of life. You may also spend most of the hours in your day physically working instead of enjoying life. The Business of Time was written to help you avoid either scenario, so you can choose to spend your time doing things that bring you joy instead of stress.

I hope you have enjoyed this book. This book was written to help people get the most out of life, while earning a comfortable living for themselves. We all have a limited amount of time on this earth and we should all be able to *enjoy* the time we are here!

Chapter Checklist

In this chapter we discussed alternate ways to earn money for yourself. Have you thought about the following to earn for yourself while you are not "physically" working?

- Have you considered how much you work in relation to how much you earn, and how that affects your overall happiness?
- Have you investigated any/all ways to make passive and/or residual income?
- Do you have a separate retirement account set up for yourself?
- Do you manage your retirement account? Is the money in your retirement account working for you while you are not working?
- If your retirement income is stock market based, are you paying attention to the stocks that you are invested in? If not, you could be adding time onto the amount of years you *need* to continue working.
- Do you feel that you have struck a good balance in life? If not, based on what you have read in this book, what lessons could you apply to help yourself feel more balanced?

A New Beginning

Now that you have read The Business of Time, I hope you have a greater understanding of the options that are available to you. In addition to what you have read in this book, I have also curated many videos on YouTube that further explain the topics discussed in this book. My YouTube channel is constantly updated, with new content to help you remain relevant in these ever-changing times that we all live in. You can subscribe to my YouTube channel (Timothy DeJesus) so you do not miss any updates, and it will not cost you any money to subscribe.

Upon saying that, I just want to say thank you very much for taking the time to read this book. I hope you have found it to be informative and educational. I wrote this book because I wanted to share the personal lessons I have learned throughout my life. I hope that by sharing, this book will help at least a few people.

The reason I talk about retirement and passive/residual income throughout this book is because again, we all have the same number of hours in a day. I personally enjoy working, but if I have a choice between working or traveling the world and/or spending time with my daughter (things that I enjoy more), I'm going to choose to spend my time doing things that I enjoy the most. I believe if you are being honest with yourself, you would choose to do the same, and you can.

The key to having the ability to choose what you would like to do with your time is to maximize your personal value, whether you work for yourself or someone else, and to also figure out ways to earn money while you are not physically working. By doing so, you can maximize your earnings during your physical working hours and begin to minimize the amount of time you need to spend physically working. When you spend less time working, you will have more time available to do things that you enjoy (provided you can support yourself financially).

Keep this in mind as well: there is no right or wrong answer when it comes to working for someone else or working for yourself. It is a matter of personal perspective that relates to your overall happiness in life. If you can work for someone else with minimal stress and earn a comfortable living, that is great. If you are working for a company that you feel does not appreciate or value you, you can also consider the option of self-employment. Keep this in mind though: you will need to find a way to replace the income that you were making while working for someone else. If you are not able to figure out how to do so, you may be better off just working for someone else until you can replace your income. If you cannot support yourself and your family, you risk adding more stress in your life by attempting to be self-employed.

The concepts discussed in this book were written with the goal of allowing you to choose what you would like to do in life. At the point that I started to write this book, I decided to not let others dictate how I would like to live my life. I did not want to be required to work late into my senior years, and I did not want to regret my choices when I was older. I hope this book allows you to do the same.

Everything that has been discussed throughout this book has led you to this point. I hope you have learned from this book and can apply the concepts you have read about to your personal situation. The goal, as stated earlier, is for you to be able to find happiness regardless of your financial earnings. Money can make life easier, but money alone typically does not buy happiness. It is up to you to decide what is most important to you, then you can begin to work on your personal goals and achieve whatever you deem success to be. Success and money do not have to be tied to one another. I wish you the best in your journey and I hope you can achieve happiness/satisfaction.

Regardless of what you have chosen to do up to this point, or what you choose to do going forward, enjoy your life. Life can be difficult, but you can get past difficult situations and have the life you believe you should have. Sometimes a small change that you make in life can yield great results. Take the time to examine your situation and determine what changes you can make to find happiness (if you are not happy/satisfied already). We all have a limited amount of time on this earth. Make the most of your time here and remember that you can, and should, enjoy life!

Printed in Great Britain
by Amazon

49440305R00061